ROM

Low Hills

For

Very Flat
and Low

KON MTS.

E

R

Low and Flats

Kolto

RIVER

ONILA

UKON

Rapids

Nuklukahyet

Towikakat

Supposed course of Tananah R.
(From Indian Reports)

d

A

ALAS

Atna or
Copper River

N MTS.

Chena River

MT. WRA

S

Creek River

Chechitn

"The proper function of man is to live, not exist.
I shall not waste my days in trying to prolong them.
I shall use my time."

JACK LONDON
Wilderness Writer

———•———

By Edward Beecher Claflin
FOREWORD BY PROFESSOR EARLE LABOR

THE KIPLING PRESS • NEW YORK

Printed in the United States
ISBN 0-943718-03-1

The Kipling Press
Second printing (revised) 1988

FOREWORD

Jack London is unique. In all of American literature, there is no other figure quite like him.

Born in 1876 during our first Centennial, London epitomizes the spirit of rugged youth and manly adventure, along with the will to succeed in the face of terrific adversity, which characterized this strenuous age in American history. It was the era of Horatio Alger and the self-made man, of Andrew Carnegie and the captains of industry, of Teddy Roosevelt and his Rough Riders. Jack London became a legend during his own lifetime and is now a permanent part of American mythology.

No American writer ever struggled against greater odds than London did. None ever fought uphill with more spectacular success, and none ever achieved wider popularity. Here are some of the facts of his extraordinary life and career:

He was born out of wedlock and never saw his natural father.

He spent his boyhood years under the constant threat of poverty and hardship.

When he finished grade school, he had to stop his formal education and assume the life of what he later called "a work beast," sweating in a cannery twelve to sixteen hours a day for ten cents an hour.

Yet, even as a boy, he found ways to escape this life of drudgery: first, through the wonderful world of books; then, through the actual adventures of hoboing, sailing, and pirating.

Here are the four ingredients that made up Jack London's philosophy of life: (1) his devotion to books, (2) his hatred of mindless labor, (3) his love of adventure, and (4) his belief in good comradeship. These same four ingredients served as themes in his writings.

In the summer of 1897, Jack got his big break: a chance to participate in the Great Klondike Gold Rush. He was just twenty-one years old. "It was in the Klondike that I found myself," Jack later remarked. "There you get your perspective. I got mine."

His new perspective enabled him to see that he had something very special to give the world as a creative writer. London had tried to start his career as a professional writer before going to the Klondike. Except for winning the twenty-five-dollar first prize in a novice writer's contest at the age of seventeen, however, he had nothing to show for his efforts but misery and rejection slips (over six hundred during the first five years of his career!). But when he got back from the Klondike in the summer of 1898, finding that his beloved stepfather, John London, had died and that the duty of supporting his family had fallen upon his own shoulders, Jack resolved to "make it" as a writer.

Within a year of his dramatic resolution, his stories had been accepted for publication by such prestigious magazines as the *Overland Monthly* and the *Atlantic Monthly*. He was also under contract with Houghton Mifflin to publish his first book, and the literary critics were acclaiming him as "the Kipling of the

Klondike." Within five years he had become internationally famous, and his masterpiece *The Call of the Wild* had achieved status as a world classic.

During the brief eighteen-year span between his 1898 resolution to succeed and his untimely death from a stroke in 1926, Jack London accomplished enough to satisfy a half-dozen normally ambitious men. He managed to support several families from his earnings as a writer. (He is reputed to have been the first writer ever to earn more than a million dollars from his pen alone.) He traveled, lectured, and wrote freely in behalf of the Socialist Party. (He was an ardent crusader for the rights of the working man and justice for the underprivileged classes.) He built and sailed his own ship, the *Snark*, halfway around the globe. He pioneered modern agricultural methods and livestock breeding, developing a model ranch in Northern California's Valley of the Moon. (Part of this ranch is now the Jack London State Historic Park.)

During this same brief period, London produced more than fifty books, four hundred nonfiction pieces, and two hundred short stories on a broad range of subjects.

Today Jack London's works are still enjoyed by readers around the globe—from Asia to Europe (including the Soviet Union, where he has long been the most popular foreign author). He is one of America's greatest writers.

> *— Earle Labor*
> *Centenary College of Louisiana*
> *October 10, 1986*

Jack London with friends (1913)

GOLD IN THE KLONDIKE

"Because men, groping in the Arctic darkness,
had found a yellow metal. . ."

Sweat and grime streaked the face of the young man on the trail. Step by step he trudged upward. His muddy boots slithered on the treacherous incline.

Ahead, the path wound its way up through the steep mountain passes and deep gullies of the Alaskan terrain. Men struggled to keep their footing on the edge of the sheer precipice, as now and then a curse was heard, followed by the whinny of a horse or mule that balked at the terrifying height.

The young man paused an instant to push back the shock of dark brown hair that drooped over his brow. He was handsome and smooth shaven, his full lips set in a grim line of determination.

Muscles strained to the bursting point, he bent forward to bear the weight of the crushing load that dragged at his shoulders.

"Look ho!" A terrified voice ahead of him cried out.

"Nyaaaahyeeeeee!"

There was a piercing shriek like an Indian war cry.

"Hold that mare! Hold her!" bellowed another voice.

Suddenly the orderly stream of men and animals turned to bedlam. A mare had lost her footing on the narrow trail and was sliding toward the edge. Oblivious to the weight on his back, and the painful exhaustion in his muscles, the young man lunged to the rescue, seizing the halter rope.

The mare's eyes rolled back in their sockets, red with terror.

"Stand clear! Stand clear!" men shouted, scrambling out of range of the terrified animal.

For an instant, the young man's vision was filled with the sight of the animal's rolling, bloodshot eyes. In that moment the mare's terror became his own. He clutched the halter tightly, straining to keep her on the trail. He dug in his heels as hard as he could, but it was no use. The five-hundred-pound load on the mare's back was dragging her down.

"Let her go!" bellowed someone from behind. "Let her go! She's a goner!"

The halter slipped from the young man's hands. He caught a final glimpse of the mare's bloodshot eyes—a look that was almost human in its final appeal.

Then the mare was gone, rolling and dashing among the stumps and boulders like a child's ball hurtling down a hillside.

A terrible quietness settled over the men on the trail.

The young man who had tried to save the mare stepped back from the edge. His arms were still trembling.

He had failed.

A moment before, the living creature had been in his hands. And then—gone. It had all happened in an instant. A moment more and he too would have plunged into the depths of the muddy gorge to lie broken among the rocks and snags. Stunned, he could not tear his gaze from the scene far below.

"Get on! Get on!" voices shouted behind him. "We haven't got all day!"

Squaring his shoulder against the one-hundred-pound weight that bent his back, the young man turned to the trail again.

But as he plodded along the mud-slicked, narrow path, his mind was elsewhere. Survival—what did that mean? What would his life be worth in the days ahead? On winter nights in barren Alaska, when the thermometer plunged to seventy degrees below zero, would he have the stamina needed to live in this vast, unforgiving wasteland?

At twenty-one years of age, Jack London knew the answer. A grueling trek ahead of him. But he had not come all this way to turn back.

He was ready for the test.

In the summer of 1897, thousands of men joined the rush to Alaska to search for gold in the Klondike. For these men headed for the frozen North, the promise of gold on the Klondike meant more than riches. It was a dream of wild escapades and bold adventure that drew these gold-seekers away from the security of their faraway homes.

In the year 1897, western expansion in the United States had almost come to an end. The mountains, streams and woodlands of the West had been crossed, climbed, charted and explored. Ever since the end of the Civil War, thirty-two years before, America had settled into a pattern of steady growth and industrialization.

Now, three years before the turn of the century, the men who were changing the face of America were no longer farmers, cattlemen, trappers, explorers and Indian fighters. Instead, they were great industrialists—men like John D. Rockefeller, Andrew Carnegie, and Cornelius Vanderbilt who had earned massive amounts of money in oil, steel, and far-flung shipping and railroad enterprises. The "capitalists" were hated as much as they were envied for their ambitious enterprises and enormous wealth.

But how could the "average American" strike it rich in those days? On the East and West coasts in the centers of industry, men, women and children sweated away ten to sixteen hours a day in dingy, oppressive factories. Across the vast Midwest, farmers toiled morning to night, battling poor soil, drought, harsh winters and grueling summers to raise crops that were sold for pennies in profit. For the past five years—from 1893 to 1897— the United States had been in the grips of its first great depression. Men and women were thrown out of work and children were sent begging in the streets. No wonder the cry of "Gold!" sent these adventurers rushing toward the Klondike. Many had spent their last dime to outfit themselves for the Yukon. Recklessly, they had left their homes and families behind to set out in search of their fortunes. What did it really matter whether they won or lost in this great gamble? Anything was better than slaving away on a factory floor for the rest of your life—or standing in the unemployment line. This was adventure to compare with the opening of the Wild West.

Gold in the Klondike! It was now or never!

O f all those toiling their way toward the Chilkoot Pass, few had the stamina of young Jack London. Though only twenty-one years of age, he had experience and wisdom beyond his years.

Born in Oakland, just outside San Francisco, on January 13, 1876, Jack had never known his true father—a wandering astrologer who hightailed it out of Oakland before Jack was born. Jack's stepfather, John London, was a Pennsylvania farmer. His mother, Flora, was a psychic who held seances in which she was guided by an Indian spirit named "Plume." Jack also had two stepsisters, Eliza and Ida, who often took care of him when he was growing up. During his early years, Jack's family moved several times, and his mother and stepfather were constantly struggling to make ends meet.

Jack could hardly remember a time when he wasn't working. By age eleven he had a regular newspaper route and he was the boy helper on an ice cream wagon. After school he found time to set up pins at the local bowling alley, and he swept out saloons at Sunday picnic grounds to earn additional pocket money.

When he graduated from grammar school at age fourteen, Jack had just a brief summer's vacation. Then he immediately started working —twelve to eighteen hours a day in a cannery, alongside children who were six or seven years old. Most of his earnings went to the family. At fifteen, he was able to buy himself an oyster boat, the *Razzle Dazzle*. Soon he was raiding oyster beds in San Francisco Bay with men like French Frank and Spider Healey and other so-called Oyster Pirates who spent their days dodging the U.S. Government Fish Patrol.

During the next five years, Jack London's life was a ceaseless round of adventure, work, ambitious plans and reckless highjinks. Switching sides, he joined the Fish Patrol, hunting down the fishermen violating fishing and game laws much in the same way as the Oyster Pirates he'd been in cahoots with before. Soon after, he joined the crew of the *Sophia Sutherland*, a three-masted schooner bound for the Bering Sea off the coast of Japan. Upon his return he took a job in a jute mill, working ten-hour days in the noisy mill where jute fiber was woven into burlap and string. During this period, he somehow found time to write his first work that was published—a prizewinning account of his adventures called "Story of a Typhoon Off the Coast of Japan." Jack won the first prize of

Jack London at the age of nine

twenty-five dollars for the story. It was printed in the *Morning Call* on November 12, 1893.

During these adventurous years, Jack did a lot of reading—and a lot of thinking. He came to the conclusion that the lives of millions of men, women and children were being destroyed by the grim oppression of factory work. When he began hearing speeches of the socialists who wanted to overturn the social order and put the

The Sophia Sutherland, *which Jack sailed to Japan*

vast capital in the hands of the very rich into the hands of all working people, his imagination caught fire. Having sweated his youth away in backbreaking toil, Jack London could see the sense in that!

He joined the ranks of "Kelly's Industrial Army," a huge assembly of jobless workers who organized a great march to protest unemployment. Jack rode the boxcars with "Kelly's Army," survived freezing nights in shabby tent-villages and learned how to tramp the roads. Eventually he left the "army" behind and made his way cross-country by boat, on foot and in railway cars. But bad luck caught up with him in Niagara Falls, New York, where he was arrested for being a hobo ("vagrancy" was the charge) and sentenced to thirty days in the miserable Erie County Penitentiary in Buffalo.

After his release from prison on July 29, 1894, he continued to tramp his way cross-country, arriving home in time to enroll in the Class of '97 at Oakland High School.

For the next two years, he studied, worked and courted a pretty, young girl named Mabel Applegarth. But when he heard about gold on the Klondike, the lure was too much. Like thousands of young men, Jack caught the gold fever.

Jack's brother-in-law, Captain Shepard, decided to join Jack in this great adventure. He mortgaged his house to buy a year's supply of "grub, mining implements, tents, blankets, Klondike stoves, everything requisite to maintain life, build boats and cabins." Loaded up with nearly two thousand pounds apiece, Jack and Captain Shepard boarded the *S.S. Umatilla* on July 25, 1897. They caught the *City of Topeka* at Port Townsend, arriving at Juneau, Alaska, on August 2. At Juneau they transferred all their luggage to seventy-foot canoes paddled by Indians. Three days later, they unloaded everything in the brawling, bustling Port of Dyea.

Just beyond the mountains that surrounded Dyea—and another five hundred miles away—lay the gold fields of the Klondike. But the way there was difficult.

A Klondike trapper (1904)

Packers ascending the summit of Chilkoot Pass (1898)

THE YUKON

" . . . Straight meat was the bill of fare, ammunition
and tools principally made up
the load on the sled, and the time
card was drawn upon the limitless future."

On October 9, 1897, Jack and his companions in the *Yukon Belle* reached Upper Island near Stewart Camp, eighty miles from Dawson. Snows covered the ground and the rivers were already freezing up, but Jack London was anxious to begin gold-hunting. With several other gold-seekers, he set out early on the morning of October 12 to dig for gold on the North Fork of Henderson Creek.

Jack didn't find any large nuggets on his first day of exploration. However, he and his companions staked eight claims on the left fork of Henderson Creek. Later, London

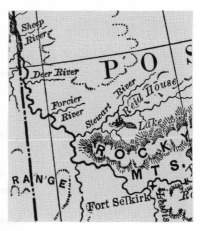

filed papers for claim No. 54 with the gold commissioner in Dawson, stating, "I solemnly swear that I have discovered therein a deposit of Gold."

On November 5, the same day Jack filed his claim, the Yukon River froze over. Jack spent another month in Dawson. Then he and a friend, Fred Thompson, made the five-day hike north to Split-up Island, where he was to spend the winter in a small cabin with a number of other gold-seekers.

December had arrived. Silence gripped the world. Outside the cabin door, snow fell steadily. Darkness settled around them. Temperatures plummeted to seventy below. Inside the cabin, men eagerly fed logs into the cast-iron stove, keeping alive the yellow blaze that was their sole protection from the frozen darkness outside their door. They talked, they smoked, they argued. They played poker, swore, bragged about their conquests with women, and debated the state of affairs in the far-off world they had come from.

Throughout the winter, Jack London frequently retired to a corner of the desolate cabin. By light of a smoky kerosene lamp, with a thick jacket around his shoulders to protect him from the creeping cold, he read the books he had brought from the "Southland."

Jack's cabin mates thought he was out of his mind. Adding weight to the burden of food and essential supplies that he had carried more than five hundred miles were the most impractical of objects for the Klondike as far as they were concerned— books! Not just one—but numerous weighty volumes. He had Darwin's *Origin of Species*, Haeckel's *Riddle of the Universe*, Milton's *Paradise Lost*, Kipling's *Seven Seas* and many others.

When he finished a book, Jack pounced on one of his friends, urging him to listen to the thrilling words he had just read. Deep

Jack London in the Klondike (1898)

in the frozen North, thousands of miles from the nearest city, young Jack London debated the great issues of his day—socialism and Darwinism, the God-given rights of human beings and the primitive origins of the human race.

Bored, dirty, unshaven—huddled around the life-giving heat of the stove—the men in the cabin shook their heads and muttered. But Jack's enthusiasm slowly won them over. He would talk for hours—about all the things in his precious books and more besides. It was wild talk, but good—full of stories, ideas and magnificent dreams.

Jack gathered some of these stories while he was hanging around the Oakland and San Francisco waterfronts, or sailing on the high seas in the South Pacific. Others came from the days when eighteen-year-old Jack rode the rails with "Kelly's Army" of unemployed.

Though the men in the cabin still made fun of his reading, they listened intently to Jack's storytelling. And some of Jack's idealistic social theories made sense to them. Why shouldn't wealth be shared equally among rich and poor, among arrogant capitalists and sweating laborers?

Here in the North, all were equal. There were no kings, no rich capitalists, no angry bosses or subservient factory hands. Class distinctions did not exist in this cold land where only the strong and fit could survive. If these men made it to spring, one of them might become a millionaire—but who could say which one? Rich or poor, educated or ignorant, all were kept alive by the flickering flame in the cast-iron stove and the sacks of food in the corner.

During his winter on the Yukon, Jack London came down with scurvy. The disease is caused by lack of vitamin C, normally supplied by a diet of fresh fruit and vegetables. It was a common affliction on the Klondike, where men survived the winter on a diet that consisted mostly of "the three-Bs"—beans, bread, and bacon.

Long before spring, Jack London had been ravaged by the disease. He was covered with sores. His gums had turned spongy and his teeth were loose. By the time he struggled into the small Catholic hospital in Dawson, he was so weak that he could hardly stand up.

Jack recovered, but as spring came to the Yukon, he remained temporarily crippled from the waist down. He could not stay in the frozen North.

As soon as the ice broke up, Jack sought passage on any boat that would take him back down the Yukon River. He was broke and could not pay for passage. Generously, a man named Prewitt gave up his place on a small boat headed downriver. Because of Jack's condition, the other two men allowed him to travel free. They made the nineteen-hundred mile trip down the Yukon in just nineteen days.

Scouring the waterfront for passage back to the States, Jack got a job as stoker on a ship bound for British Columbia. From British Columbia, he traveled steerage class to Seattle on a passenger boat. On the last leg of the journey he boarded a freight train bound for Oakland.

A little less than a year after his departure, Jack London stood at the door of his mother's house. He was home again. He had failed to make his fortune in the frozen gold fields of the Klondike. But now he had a new aim—Jack London wanted to be a writer.

Jack at his California ranch (circa 1915)

JACK LONDON, WRITER

"There is an ecstasy that marks the summit of life,
and beyond which life cannot rise. . ."

In years to come, the stories that Jack London composed about the Yukon would bring him more money than any of the promised gold. After he returned to San Francisco in 1898, Jack began to write furiously about the sights, characters, and adventures of the North.

In the first rush of words that spilled from Jack London's pen there emerged pictures of wild adventure and haunting scenery. He captured the bleakness, danger and horror of men who were caught in the grip of the subarctic cold.

During his Klondike winter, Jack London had stared blankly into the darkness, listened to a silence so vast there was no relief, and witnessed the fragility of life. Reading Darwin's *Origin of Species*, he had thought long and deeply about the implications of Darwin's theories.

Among human beings, as other animals, only the fit would survive. Sometimes it was the law of the jungle: kill or be killed. Other times, it was simply man against nature: find warmth, shelter and food—or perish. But always, the formula was the same. To conquer the specter of death took wits, strength and courage. Even when luck was in his favor, a man's life could end suddenly and without warning.

This struggle for survival was to be the central theme of all Jack London's writing.

In *To Build a Fire*, written five years later in 1907, the enemy is not human. It is the arctic cold creeping over the man who struggles to survive:

> *A certain fear of death, dull and oppressive, same to him. This fear quickly became poignant as he realized that it was no longer a mere matter of freezing his fingers and toes, or of losing his hands and feet, but that it was a matter of life and death with the chances against him.*

When Jack London wrote these words, he was a well-known author, writing from the security of his study in Oakland. But his memories of the Yukon remained keen and vivid. Every word that he put on paper helped to bring those memories alive—of the bitter cold, the terror of the darkness, the frost and the silence. Once again he found himself in the vast reaches of the North, where dog and man struggled for survival against almost insurmountable odds.

But the Yukon, as Jack London portrayed it, was the work of

his imagination as well as his memory. To portray Buck, the sled dog in *Call of the Wild*, Jack London had to imagine what it was like to use a dog's instincts, to survive the brutality of cruel men, and to fight hunger-crazed animals of his own kind.

In *To Build A Fire*, Jack London managed an even greater feat of the imagination by putting himself in the place of a dying man and the animal that observes him. As the man realizes that his hour has come, his last hope gone, he sinks into the comforting numbness of death while his dog watches:

> *Then the man drowsed off into what seemed to him the most comfortable and satisfying sleep he had ever known. The dog sat facing him and waiting. The brief day drew to a close in a long, slow twilight. There were no signs of a fire to be made, and, besides, never in the dog's experience had it known a man to sit like that in the snow and make no fire. As the twilight drew on, its eager yearning for the fire mastered it, and with a great lifting and shifting of forefeet, it whined softly, then flattened its ears down in anticipation of being chidden by the man. But the man remained silent.*

For a young man of twenty-two who desperately wanted to be a writer, the next two years were as great a test as anything he experienced in the Yukon. Jack had proven his strength and nerves against the forces of nature. Now it was time to prove himself in the society of men and women who would measure him by his words. He had to write—but more than that, he had to become a published author.

How? He had no connections in the literary world. He didn't associate with powerful editors who could give him assignments or pay advances for his stories. Furthermore, the stories he wanted to write didn't fit the mold.

The great American literary giants of the late nineteenth cen-

Rudyard Kipling

Samuel Clemens (Mark Twain)

tury, men like Mark Twain, William Dean Howells and Henry James, were already fading in popularity. Now publishers were looking for novels that had plenty of "sentiment and swordplay" to satisfy a public that was beginning to buy books by the millions.

Jack was not prepared to write stories like that. But he was certain that people would read realistic stories of everyday heroism and adventure, if only he could get his stories published.

Jack was penniless when he got back from Alaska. Now he needed money to support his mother and himself while he got on with his writing. But the only jobs he could find were menial—cutting lawns and hedges, cleaning windows and beating carpets. For a young man who had ventured on the high seas and shared grub with the gold-seekers on the Klondike, these odd jobs were a dead end.

What else could he do? If he were to write, he had to make a living until his writing could support him.

In 1898, many magazines were publishing adventure stories. Jack poured over magazines like *The Youth's Companion* and *Overland Monthly*, trying to discover what kinds of stories the editors would like. He analyzed each story to discover what made it publishable. All the time he was writing furiously, staying up beyond midnight to finish a story, then leaping from his bed at dawn to begin writing again. He spent all his extra pennies on stamps and envelopes. As soon as a story was finished, he sent it off. Week after week, rejection notes arrived in the mail.

His life became increasingly frenzied. What was wrong? Why didn't the editors take his stories? Why didn't they like his work? He turned to Rudyard Kipling's stories, copying them page by page in longhand. By steadily copying line after line, perhaps Jack London would develop the habit of writing well—as well as Kipling, thrilling his readers.

Meanwhile, day by day, the necessity of providing for himself and his mother steadily wore him down. He also now had to provide for another addition to the family—John Miller, the son of his stepsister Eliza Miller. The boy became known as "Little John." Jack loved him, but it was hard having another to feed.

Finally, even the girl he loved turned against him.

Before he went away to the Klondike, Jack had called frequently on pretty Mabel Applegarth—the sister of one of his best friends, Ted Applegarth.

For a time, Jack was very much in love. But after he returned from the Klondike, he gradually became aware that Mabel did not have the slightest understanding of who he was or what he wanted.

When Mabel read his stories, she shook her head in dismay. To this proper young woman with delicate manners, Jack's stories seemed crude and unpleasant. His characters talked rough and acted like brutes. They cursed their sled dogs and beat them into submission. Their only law was the law of nature—kill or be killed. On the brink of starvation they ate their own animals.

Jack's stories depressed her. She could not understand why a handsome, charming young man like Jack was attracted to life's ugliness.

She urged him to give up his writing and get a steady job. Perhaps he could become a postman, she suggested. All he had to do was pass the post office examination.

Jack's mother Flora, his stepsister, Eliza, and Mabel's mother, all agreed with Mabel. "What is Jack going to accomplish with his writing?" they asked. He wasted his days and nights at his desk, scribbling stories about bloodshed and violence. He was ruining his health, driving himself mercilessly. For what purpose? The rejections kept piling up—each more devastating than the last—each only spurring him to further efforts. Why did he refuse to listen to reason?

All their doubts began to have an effect on Jack. In spite of his stubbornness, he started to bow under the pressure. Maybe Mabel was right. Maybe he should settle down and stop wasting his time with this writing business.

At Mabel's urging, Jack took the civil service examination for the post office. But even as he waited for the results, he was filled with dread. What if he passed the exam? What if he actually became a postman? The mere thought of it made him cringe.

Jack London was a writer! No one else believed it. But he did. He had to!

Finally, in early December of 1898, a long envelope arrived on Jack's doorstep. The letter was from *Overland Monthly*, a prestigious Western magazine that had been edited by the famous Bret Harte, author of such stories as "The Luck of Roaring Camp" and "The Outcasts of Poker Flat."

Jack seized the envelope, ripped it open, and yanked out the letter.

The story, "To the Man on the Trail" was accepted. It would be published in the January issue!

Jack let out a whoop. Leaping to his feet, he waved the letter triumphantly in the air. That was it! This proved it!

The acceptance from *Overland Monthly* came none too soon. It is hard to say how much longer the idealistic young man could hold out against the pressures placed on him.

On the other hand, one acceptance did not make Jack London's future any clearer or easier.

After all, where did a wild, adventurous writer with socialist ideas fit on the literary scene of the day? His energetic style and the powerful realism of his stories were like nothing American readers were seeing in those days.

Of course, Jack had no idea that he was soon to ride the crest of a new wave of American writing, called "Naturalism." In later years, literary critics would see Jack London as part of the movement that included other young writers like Hamlin Garland,

Stephen Crane and Frank Norris. Each in his own way, brought a new awareness of social injustices and the cruelty of nature.

But the young Jack London was far from a "man of letters." And in his early days as a writer, he dealt daily with the endless problems of poverty.

Payment for his first story was pitifully small—just five dollars for a story that had taken him nearly five days to write. Also, acceptance by one publication did not mean that his stories would automatically be taken by others. So he would still have to work at menial jobs even while he was writing.

Nor did publication guarantee him favor in the eyes of gentle-minded readers like Mabel Applegarth.

A position opened up at the Post Office, but Jack turned it down. Mabel showed her disappointment in him. Why should he continue in his wild, reckless ways —writing crude stories of Alaska for a few dollars here and there—when he could settle down to a steady line of work?

Jack could not answer her—because he did not know the answer. He only knew that writing had been his lifeblood. He dreamed of riches, but becoming a successful writer now meant as much to him as money.

Mabel was a kind of ideal woman, embodying everything that was gentle, beautiful and romantic. But if Jack took a permanent job and married Mabel he would be finished as a writer.

Torn by conflicting feelings, Jack lashed out at Mabel. She misunderstood him completely, he claimed. In his bitterness, he wrote her, "In a general, vaguely general way, you know my aspirations, but of the real Jack, his thoughts, feelings, etc., you are positively ignorant."

It was a harsh, angry letter, written on impulse. But it was true.

Mabel did not understand him—she never would. Trying to reconcile their differences was hopeless. He could not detach himself from the ideals of love that she represented. But he knew he had to tear himself away from his dreams and illusions about sharing a life with her.

Jack London might be many things. But he was not a postman, and he never would be.

Jack London and his second wife Charmian

A SETTLED LIFE

"Dis is de las'. Den we get one long res'.
Eh? For sure. One bully long res'."

Relentlessly, Jack London pursued his goal. Encouraged by his success with the *Overland Monthly*, he submitted stories to a long list of magazines. The tide began to turn in his favor. Readers loved his stories of wild adventure. His first stories, published in the *Overland Monthly*, had alluring titles that captivated readers— "To the Man on the Trail," "The White Silence," and "The Son of the Wolf." The world they described was equally alluring. Letters of acceptance replaced the rejection slips that had filled his mailbox.

By 1900, Jack's stories, as well as a few essays, had been published in

Mclure's, The Black Cat, Cosmopolitan and—far more prestigious than all the rest—*Atlantic Monthly*. Best of all, a collection of his stories was accepted for publication by Houghton Mifflin and Co. of Boston. The book came out with the title *The Son of the Wolf*. Houghton Mifflin's reader, who first recommended the stories for publication, wrote the following report on Jack London: "He uses the current slang of the mining camps a little too freely, but his style has freshness, vigor and strength. The reader is convinced that the author has lived the life himself."

At last publishers were beginning to understand what Jack was trying to accomplish. He had lived the life. It was not a pretty existence. But his fiction conveyed a "vivid picture of the terrors of cold, darkness and starvation."

Soon, all across America, readers were picking up their favorite magazines and looking for Jack London's thrilling stories. He gathered a following. In the comfort of their living rooms, on warm summer nights with cool drinks in hand, readers picked up Jack London's tales. Instantly, they were transported to a barren wasteland at the extreme edge of the world, where man and beast fought for survival. Without ever leaving the comfort of their homes, people felt what it was like to be far away on a Klondike adventure. They hungered for more.

There was another side to Jack London that interested an ever-growing American audience. He was a social reformer. One of his essays, published in *Cosmopolitan*, was called "What Communities Lose by the Competitive System." Here Jack spoke out on one of his favorite subjects—socialism. Competition caused waste and inefficiency, he declared. What was needed in America was a planned society, where the burdens of labor and the rewards of wealth would be shared equally.

The essay eloquently reviewed some of the principles that Jack London had been declaring for a long time. Though not a great speaker, he had often voiced his opinions at socialist meetings in Oakland and other towns and cities.

Socialism, for Jack London, was a political theory that promised hope for millions of people. He had studied Karl Marx's *Capital* (first published in English in 1877) and he agreed with many of Marx's theories. As Jack saw it, there was clearly a conflict between capitalists (the men who held the purse strings) and labor (the men, women and children who worked with machines). If there were any justice in the world, the rewards of capital and labor should be shared equally!

Books, self-education, and writing had proved to be an escape for Jack London. But what would become of people who had little or no education? They could only work slavishly in industries that consumed their energy, ground them down, and then turned them out on the streets to fend for themselves. In the early 1900s there were no protections such as minimum wage laws, pensions, public health care or Social Security. The employed as well as the unemployed had to fend for themselves. The industrial age had come to America. Society was remaking itself. But as Jack London saw it, the only law that applied was still the law of the jungle.

Now that he had gained a reputation as an ambitious author and a social activist, Jack London's fame grew by leaps and bounds. He was quoted in the newspapers. His stories and essays were passed from hand to hand. His reputation preceded him. Oyster pirate, sea voyager, Klondike adventurer, spokesman of the poor—at twenty-four, the energetic young man with the ready grin was a boy wonder.

The world lay at his doorstep. And still, he was dissatisfied.

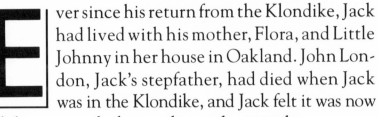

Ever since his return from the Klondike, Jack had lived with his mother, Flora, and Little Johnny in her house in Oakland. John London, Jack's stepfather, had died when Jack was in the Klondike, and Jack felt it was now his responsibility to care for his mother and stepnephew.

As soon as he could afford it, Jack, his mother, and Little Johnny moved to a larger, two-story house at 1130 East Fifteenth Street in Oakland. During the move, Flora, Little Johnny and Jack were helped by a handsome, bustling young woman named Bessie Maddern. Jack and Bessie had been friends for many years, but no one was prepared for the surprise announcement that Jack was soon to make.

Jack had asked Bessie to marry him!

The marriage was set for April 7, 1900, which coincided with the publication date of *The Son of the Wolf*.

Flushed with victory at being a real author, Jack London decided that he could start a family without jeopardizing his writing career. With Bessie, Jack felt himself in the comfortable presence of a woman who would be a steadfast wife and good mother. Writing to a friend, Jack London explained his sudden decision:

> *I made up my mind. Sunday evening I opened transactions for a wife; and next Sunday morning I shall marry Bessie Maddern. I shall be steadied, and can be able to devote more time to my work. One only has one life, after all, and why not live it? Besides, my heart is large, and I shall be a cleaner, wholesomer man because of a restraint being laid up on me instead of being free to drift wheresoever I listed. I am sure you will understand.*

Bessie, too, probably understood her role from the very beginning of their marriage. She knew that Jack was consumed by his writing and his social causes. She also knew that he was not passionately in love with her—because he told her so! He believed, he said, in a scientific, unsentimental approach to marriage. Yet it was not long before Bessie began to love *him*.

Life with Jack London was a constant whirlwind of events. Surrounded by friends, social activists and aspiring writers, he would often invite near strangers—and even perfect strangers—to his dinner table. He spent freely and loaned money to his friends. *The Son of the Wolf* was a huge popular success, and Jack anticipated enormous royalties. After the years of hard work, struggle and sacrifice, it was exhilarating to realize his dreams at last. He thought the money would keep pouring in. As a result, he overspent and was constantly in debt—a pattern that would continue throughout his life.

In 1901, Jack and Bessie London had their first child. To Jack's disappointment, it was a girl. They named her Joan.

In 1902, a second child, Becky, was born. Again Jack had wanted a son—but he did not dwell on regrets. Instead, he buried himself in his work, steadily writing one thousand words a day.

Two more books were published—a second collection of Klondike stories called *The God of His Fathers* and a first novel, *A Daughter of the Snows*. The story collection was well received, but even Jack considered *A Daughter of the Snows* a failure. He had tried to make a female character a heroine in the novel, but while his portrait of her was true in many details, it was not convincing to most readers.

The year Becky was born, Jack moved his family to a larger home in the Piedmont Hills near Oakland. Every week Jack invited dozen of people to the new house. He expected them to be fed and entertained, but Bess was more interested in caring for her girls than in looking after all of Jack's friends.

Jack thought he would be a "clearer, wholesomer man" because of the restraints marriage placed on him. But he could not change his restlessness.

Once again, he wanted to cast himself adrift. He hungered for new experiences. The furious writing he had done since returning from the Klondike had left him drained. Despite the vocation he had chosen for himself, Jack could not bear being trapped in a narrow, book-lined study.

Just when he might have settled down, he wanted to break free. The *ideal* of a quiet family life had appealed to him, but in reality that life was a noose around his neck.

THE PEOPLE OF THE ABYSS

"Life steamed through him in splendid flood,
glad and rampant, until it seemed that
it would burst asunder in sheer ecstasy. . ."

On July 21, 1902, Jack London got an assignment from the American Press Association that gave him the perfect escape. The Boer War between the South Africans and the British had just ended. Jack was asked to travel to South Africa to write about postwar conditions.

Jack eagerly accepted the assignment. He planned to travel to New York and then take a ship across the Atlantic. Before he left, however, Jack learned that the South African trip had been cancelled. He decided to go

Children from London's East End, wearing trousers made
from walnut bags (circa 1910)

East anyway, to meet with George Brett, his editor at Macmillan and Company.

Inevitably their conversation turned to Jack's next book, and they found themselves discussing social conditions in England. Soon Jack had an assignment.

"Why don't you write about the slums in the East End of London?" Brett suggested. Posing as a stranded American sailor, Jack could live in the slum and observe what life was really like among the poverty-stricken masses in England. He would then write a book upon his experiences.

The prospect was exciting. Enough dining-room debate over social theories! Jack London was ready to face the gritty reality. Once again, he would write about what he saw and experienced. The East End of London, with its filthy, overcrowded tenements, its squalor and crime, was as great a challenge as the frozen Klondike.

From this assignment came *The People of the Abyss*, one of Jack's greatest works, published in 1903 by Macmillan.

When he went into the East End, Jack had expected to see the worst. But nothing prepared him for what he actually witnessed:

> *We went up the narrow gravelled walk. On the benches on either side was arrayed a mass of miserable and distorted humanity.*
>
> *. . . It was a welter of rages and filth, of all manner of loathsome skin diseases, open sores, bruises, grossness, indecency, leering monstrosities and bestial faces. A chill, raw wind was blowing, and these creatures huddled there in their rags, sleeping for the most part, or trying to sleep. . .*
>
> *It was the sleep that puzzled me. Why were nine out of ten of them asleep or trying to sleep? But it was not till after-*

wards that I learned. It is a law of the powers that be that the homeless shall not sleep by night. . .

Throughout *The People of the Abyss* there is a tone of moral outrage. Jack London was shocked by what he saw. He tried to experience it all—the breadlines, the workhouses, the tenements, the life on the street where derelicts sorted through garbage for discarded bones and crusts of bread.

It was overwhelming. At night, he often retreated to a room he had rented in the neighborhood where the infamous "Jack the Ripper" had once lived. He made notes of his observations and tried to sleep off the nightmares that he lived through by day.

The images in *The People of the Abyss* are lasting and powerful. And each observation reinforced Jack London's belief in socialism. Things must change—they had to change. Human beings could not be allowed to live like this!

The People of the Abyss meant a great deal to Jack London personally—more, perhaps, than any of his Alaskan tales. In later years he would write:

Of all my books, I love most The People of the Abyss. *No other book of mine took so much of my young heart and tears as that study of the economic degradation of the poor.*

THE SNARK

"He was beaten (he knew that); but he was not broken."

Returning to Oakland, Jack set to work revising *The People of the Abyss* for publication with Macmillan.

He had promised George Brett that he would also produce a 4,000-word Klondike story to include in a new collection. In a previous story published in *Cosmopolitan*, Jack had portrayed the Yukon from a sled dog's point of view. Now he wanted to try it again, telling the entire story of a dog named Buck and his battle for survival in the Northland. The title was *The Call of the Wild*. But when he sat down to write, the story ran away with him. A tale of hardship and brutality, of surly men and ferocious dogs playing out a battle for survival against the harsh landscape of the Klondike, *The Call of the Wild* began to take on the form of a

lyrical epic. Jack London was pursuing his usual themes. But this time, all the details of Buck's existence came into sharp focus. As the words poured from Jack London's pen, the story refused to stay within the confines of its planned length. When he finally stopped writing, *The Call of the Wild* was more than 42,000 words. He had written the entire story in exactly one month.

Charmian (center), Jack and friends before the Snark set sail

Looking for fast money, Jack was overjoyed when the *Saturday Evening Post* paid seven hundred and fifty dollars for the rights to *The Call of the Wild* in serial form. Macmillan offered to buy the novel outright for two thousand dollars, and said the publishing house would extensively promote it. Jack immediately accepted the deal. It meant he wouldn't get any royalties in the future, but he would not quibble. He needed the money now.

First published in the *Saturday Evening Post*, then as a book, *The Call of the Wild* became the most popular of Jack London's tales. Eventually more than seven million copies would be sold. But because he earned no royalties on the book, Jack's only income on *The Call of the Wild* was the money he received initially from the *Post* and from Macmillan.

In 1903 when *The Call of the Wild* was published, the book was immediately hailed as an American classic. The first edition, ten thousand copies, sold out on the first day of publication. Jack London had become the most popular writer of his day.

Publication of *The Call of the Wild* skyrocketed Jack London to fame. But this new fame only gave him greater freedom to write more, travel more, and taste greater adventures. During the next thirteen years he lived at a frantic and exciting pace, glorying in each new achievement.

What remained consistent, however, was the enormous productivity of his fluent pen. No matter where he traveled, no matter how desperate his finances or his personal affairs, he kept writing. . .and writing and writing. In the next eighteen years, he produced over fifty books.

The year 1903 was not only a turning point in his life as a published author, it was also a year of great change in his personal life. Late in July of that year, Jack announced to Bessie that he was leaving her and his daughters. Shortly after, he moved into a six-room apartment that he shared with friends in Oakland.

The reason for this abrupt change was that Jack had fallen in love with another woman, Charmian Kittredge, an adventurous, well-read, vivacious woman, five years older than Jack.

Early in 1904, on assignment to Hearst's newspaper, Jack traveled to Japan and Korea to report on the Russo-Japanese war. Surviving a perilous trip across the Yellow Sea in a Korean junk, he nearly died of exposure before reaching the Korean mainland. Once there, Jack offended all the embassies by entering territory where correspondents were not allowed.

Upon his return from Japan, Jack was served divorce papers "on the grounds of desertion."

On November 11, 1904, Bessie was granted an "interlocutory decree of divorce," which meant that Jack would be free to marry after a one-year waiting period. Jack and Charmain were married exactly one year later.

Although Jack continued to support Bessie and his daughters he never regretted his decision to marry Charmian. Through her, he discovered a marriage could be more than a practical arrangement. In almost every way she was the perfect match for him. She loved to sail, hike, ride horseback, play the piano and take part in the rousing parties Jack enjoyed with his friends. Charmian had learned typing and shorthand and she soon took on the duties of typing Jack's manuscripts and sorting out his correspondence. From the time of their marriage in 1905 until Jack's death in 1916, Charmian was his closest companion as well as his wife. She shared his enthusiasms and was willing to take part in every adventure. When Jack was overtaken by illness in later years Charmian never left his side.

Having shocked society and made banner newspaper headlines with his marriage to Charmian, Jack proceeded to offend the socialists by buying a 129-acre estate in Glen Ellen in the Sonoma Valley. A year later, he began building a new boat, the *Snark*, that he designed himself. He planned to sail around the world with Charmian and a small crew.

Building the *Snark* was a fiasco. Supervisors, workers and suppliers all cheated him. The boat's cost doubled and redoubled. Soon after the keel was laid, the 1906 earthquake struck San Francisco and the entire boat had to be built under post-earthquake conditions.

But Jack remained grimly determined and he remained busy. During this time he wrote *The Iron Heel*, a novel which embodied all of Jack's socialist ideas and worldly experiences. He launched the *Snark* at the end of 1906. In April 1907, with Charmian and a small crew, he set sail for Hawaii.

During the passage across the Pacific, Jack climbed up to the pitching foredeck everyday to write another thousand words on his next novel, *Martin Eden*. One of his greatest works, it described the struggles of a young writer much like Jack London himself.

During its twenty-seven-month voyage, the *Snark* visited Hawaii, the Marquesas, Tahiti and the Solomon Islands. During this voyage Jack was overcome with a strange malady. His hands and feet swelled, and layer after layer of his skin peeled off. He visited doctors in Sydney, but they could not diagnose the disease. (Later on, after returning to Glen Ellen, Jack would learn that he had suffered from "sun sickness.") Jack spent several weeks recovering before returning home.

Jack London, Outdoorsman

WOLF HOUSE

> ". . .It was the dead-tiredness that comes
> through the slow and prolonged
> drainage of months of toil."

I n 1910 Jack London began a new enterprise—on land this time. This was farming. Following the advice of agricultural experts, he planted more than 150,000 eucalyptus trees on his "beauty ranch" in Glen Ellen, California. The eucalyptus trees thrived, but as it turned out there was no market for them. Jack lost his entire fifty-thousand-dollar investment.

Since 1906, Jack had harbored dreams of another mammoth project. He wanted to build a huge stone and timber mansion called Wolf House. Work on Wolf House began when Jack was already thousands of dollars in debt.

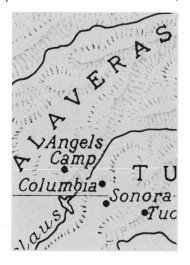

Three years later, the dream of Wolf House came to an abrupt end. Just as the building was nearing completion, Jack woke up one night to shouts of "Fire! Fire!" Flames shot up from the timbered roof and frame of the enormous structure.

Many called it sabotage. They speculated that a disgruntled socialist had set the house ablaze to punish Jack for his arrogance in building such a mansion. Later, it was determined that the fire had been caused by spontaneous combustion.

Jack swore he would rebuild Wolf House from the ground up. But it was not to be. He had too many debts and obligations. He was still supporting Bess and his two daughters, as well as the large household that he and Charmian managed. In addition, many friends had discovered that Jack London was an "easy touch." They borrowed from him constantly. When Jack asked for repayment of the loans, most of them shrugged their shoulders.

Asked to report on the Mexican Revolution for *Collier's*, Jack further angered the socialists by publishing articles against the revolution. His disputes with the socialists became more and more heated. Finally, in March 1916, Jack resigned from the Socialist Party "because of its lack of fire and fight, and its loss of emphasis on the class struggle."

Though he continued to write, he now suffered from uremia, a condition of excess urea in the blood caused by kidney disease. He and Charmian took a passenger liner to Hawaii, hoping that his health would improve.

Jack spent much of 1915 and 1916 in Hawaii. But by July 1916 when Jack and Charmian returned to Glen Ellen, it was apparent that his health was not improving.

On November 21, 1916, Jack spent the day in his study at Glen Ellen, planning a trip to New York that he intended to take soon. He sent a short note to his daughter, Joan, inviting her and her mother to have lunch with him the next day at Saddle Rock—"and, if weather is good, go for a sail with me on Lake Merrit."

But that night, Jack suffered a stroke. His heart gave out and by morning he was in a coma. Four doctors rushed to his bedside. They lifted him to his feet and walked him around, trying to restore consciousness. Jack never came out of the coma.

The newspapers carried the headlines on Thursday morning, November 23, 1916: Jack London, the most famous author of his day, was dead at the age of forty.

Today, Jack London is well-known for the great Alaskan tales *Call of the Wild* and *White Fang*. Many of his short stories are considered classics, including "All Gold Canyon," "In a Far Country," "An Odyssey of the North" and "To Build a Fire." Among the best of his works are his short story collection *On the Makeloa Mat*, his semi-autobiographical novel, *Martin Eden*, and his great sea adventure, *The Sea-Wolf*.

The People of the Abyss is a great social document, anticipating by many years the daring reporting of George Orwell in *Down and Out in London and Paris*. Though many writers deplore poverty, few have the stamina to live day after day in the grim world of the poor.

The Iron Heel, the book that Jack wrote in 1906–1907, was an out-and-out socialist novel. Years after Jack London's death, it would be highly praised by readers who saw in it the prophecy of social upheaval and change.

When Jack's writing failed, as it did in some of the novels that dealt with romance and large social issues, it was because he lost the focus and immediacy that gave his descriptions of the wilderness such power. Without this focus, his passion became mere sentimentalism.

Many of his books have never been out of print. It is a tribute to the mind and spirit of Jack London that the stories which gripped his readers in the early years of this century still have a powerful hold over us today.

In many of his novels and stories, Jack London made a powerful statement about survival in society as well as in the rough wilderness. He knew what happened when human or animal existence was reduced to its simplest terms. When the fragile structure of manners dissolved, each person had to fend for himself.

Wherever he turned, whatever his experiences, Jack London always saw this elemental struggle taking place. It narrowed the themes of his stories, but it broadened the universality of his message.

As his words carry us into the frozen North where darkness descends and the temperature plummets to seventy degrees below zero—where nothing surrounds us but bleak silence—we can learn, as his characters learned, to value the fragile life preserved like the glow of a single flame on a barren planet.

Jack London was there. He learned what it took to survive. His greatest stories were not only reminiscent of his own struggle in the Klondike, but prophetic of the struggle of all people on earth for all time to come.

A Selected Reading List

Books by Jack London

The Call of the Wild
The Cruise of the Dazzler
The Sea-Wolf
White Fang
The Star Rover
Tales of the Fish Patrol

Books About Jack London

(These books are for advanced readers.)
California Writers: Jack London & John Steinbeck—The Tough Guys, by Stoddard
  Martin, St. Martin's, 1985
Jack London, by Earle Labor, G. K. Hall, 1977
Jack London: An American Myth, by John Perry, Nelson-Hall, 1981
Jack London: Adventures, Ideas & Fiction, by James Lundquist, Ungar, 1987